Hotel del
Coronado

PUBLISHED BY THE HOTEL DEL CORONADO
CORONADO, CALIFORNIA

TABLE OF
CONTENTS

(Opposite): At the turn of the century, the Ocean Terrace was a favorite spot to relax and enjoy the ocean view.

HOTEL OF
VISIONARIES

The Hotel del Coronado has been in existence for more than a century, and yet, there have been only six owners. From Elisha Babcock, Jr., the first, to present owner M. Larry Lawrence, all have been men of vision, insight and energy.

In 1884, when Babcock was thirty-six, he came to San Diego from Evansville, Indiana, with his wife, Isabel, and their sons. He had been a railroad executive, forced into early retirement because of poor health. Though San Diego was little more than a sleepy port, Babcock saw that the area had great potential as a place where people could go to escape from the harsh Eastern winters.

Babcock and his good friend, H.L. Story (of the Story and Clark Piano Company, Chicago), spent much time hunting on the wild Coronado peninsula, across the bay from San Diego. The only access was by boat, so the two hunters rowed more than a mile in order to reach the brush-covered jut of land in their search of jackrabbit, cottontail and quail. Looking out across the open sea, opposite flat, barren land, the two men began to dream of the possibilities offered by this unique stretch of real estate.

With the railroad promising soon to reach California's southern most city and the United States' farthest corner, both Babcock and Story recognized an opportunity to lure people from all over the country to San Diego's wonderful climate, balmy Pacific breezes, quiet harbor and lush countryside. If Babcock and Story could enjoy this garden spot for hunting and fishing, then surely could those in Eastern cities, who longed to travel West while still retaining some semblance of civilization, culture and comfort.

Some might want to settle in San Diego permanently. However, the two men recognized because of its remoteness and its lack of full services and communications, many simply would want to make the area a temporary destination for resting from the rigors of life in the big cities, and for escaping from the colder climates.

Babcock and Story began to ponder how best to take advantage of the opportunities that lay before them. The onslaught of travelers surely would come—and soon.

They formed a syndicate and called it the Coronado Beach Company. Its goal was to buy the peninsula and develop it into a city. From the profits of this enterprise, a magnificent resort hotel could be built, one that would attract visitors from around the world.

(Opposite): In the early 1900s, the hotel still maintained two separate front entrances.

Ground-breaking ceremonies for The Del took place in 1887 (above).

In 1885, when the first transcontinental railroad opened the way to Barstow in the Mojave Desert, some 150 miles north, the two men made their move. They purchased the entire Coronado peninsula for $110,000.

Services had to be provided if they were to attract any people at all to this flat land filled with little else but sagebrush. A pipeline was laid from San Diego's Old Town in order to bring water from the San Diego River. A transportation system of ferryboats, wharves and even steam engine trains was installed. The sagebrush was cleared, streets were laid out and trees were planted. Electricity was virtually unknown in California, but foresight led the two men to build one of the state's first power plants. The plant would not only furnish power for their future hotel, but also to the entire city of Coronado until 1922. Another new invention, the telephone, became a part of the planned community. And a railroad extension was planned that would run along the eastern harbor shore to the south end of the bay and up the thin peninsula known as the Silver Strand.

A promotional campaign was begun. A number of Eastern newspapers carried daily San Diego temperatures, which made it the only California city, other than San Francisco, to be so honored. Rand McNally, the Chicago-based publisher, put out a booklet which heralded the advantages of life in Coronado. Meanwhile, in the city of Coronado, a pavilion was erected and regular parties were given in which wives Isabel Babcock and Della Story held court. On July 4, 1886, a great picnic celebration was held, beginning a Coronado tradition which continues to this day.

As interest developed in their planned community, Babcock and Story shifted their thoughts to the creation of a central theme for Coronado: a place where travelers could gather to relax, hunt, fish or even ponder an investment in the young city. Babcock said he wanted to create a hotel—a resort—which would become "the talk of the Western world."

Although Babcock and Story selected the Reid Brothers as architects for their wondrous dream resort, at least one designer was brought in to submit ideas before the former railroad architects arrived. Clinton Day's design was called "ornamental and striking" in a San Diego *Union* column (November 13, 1886), concluding that "the entire plan is one of beauty."

The same day the *Union* column appeared, some 6000 people (about half the population of San Diego) lined up for a free boat ride across the bay to the Coronado Beach Company's free picnic lunch, which also served as a pitch offering people a chance to invest in the new community. The terms were: one-third down, balance due in twelve months at ten percent interest. No discounts were given for cash. An ad announcing the land auction read:

> *The object of the auction of Coronado Beach property is to make a basis for prices on the unsold portions. At the close of the auction, property having the same relative location will be advanced twenty-five percent above prices obtained at the auction. This positively assures a handsome profit on any investment.*

Fortunately, it was a time of abundant money supply and no government regulations.

Prospective investors disembarked from boats at the northern tip of the peninsula (near the end of present-day Orange Avenue). They boarded railroad cars and were taken for a slow look at what must have been a wondrous sight: the once brush-covered hunter's paradise had been transformed into a genteel Eden. Markers indicated where planned streets and green shrubs would replace the once dominant sagebrush.

Orange Avenue, which remains today the city's main thoroughfare, was laced down the center with a double row of orange trees. At Sixth Avenue, the trains slowed in order to show off the new town plaza. Passengers could see palms lining Palm Avenue and olive trees decorating Olive Avenue.

Brochures emphasized Coronado's climate and soil and its ability to grow exotic ornamental plants year-round as well as lush vegetable gardens. (The sales literature, however, failed to note that alcoholic beverages were forbidden in Coronado. The Hotel del Coronado, at the beginning anyway, had a monopoly on the sale of liquor.)

As the train neared the narrow spot of the peninsula where the Silver Strand begins, passengers disembarked and crowded into a large tent for the promised free lunch and land auction. The lunch was adequate, but the auction was lively indeed.

Born into an infant community with few services, the hotel had to be self-sufficient from the beginning. It had its own power plant, laundry facilities, and foundry (above). Railroad and ferry-boat systems were built to transport lumber, building materials, fixtures and furnishings, and of course, passengers (below).

(Above): The first men of vision: E. S. Babcock, railroad man from Evansville, Indiana (far left); H. L. Story, piano magnate from Chicago (second from left); and Alonzo Horton, father of new San Diego (white beard).

(Right): Hotel—south front, 1924.

(Opposite): Elisha S. Babcock, c. 1900.

The day was a success, just as Babcock and Story had hoped. By 4 p.m., they had recouped their initial investment; they were on their way to amassing a huge profit which would be used to build their dream resort. The San Diego *Union* took note of the occasion:

> *The sale was highly satisfactory to the salesmen and to the owners and the prices brought far above what everyone had dared to fix as the limit. One shrewd real estate man said: "I expected to see those lots go for $200 on an average, but bless my stars, these prices just rattle me."*

The choice ocean-view lots went for as much as $1600 and, out of 285 properties sold on November 13 and 14, 1886, only twenty-two went for less than $200.

With enough money to begin serious planning and even construction, Babcock telegraphed the Reid Brothers, back in Evansville, Indiana; they were still working for the railroad from which Babcock had retired.

When James, Merritt, and Watson Reid made their way West, they were reminded more than once that they were traveling through untamed America. (At one point, a sheriff's posse boarded the train, riding to the next town to capture a bandit.)

James Reid would later recall the brothers' first glimpse of Coronado: "The next day, such a one as may be found only in Coronado in December, we all visited the beach. No finer location could have been found anywhere."

Like hundreds of thousands of visitors who followed them, the Reid Brothers had no desire to leave. They looked upon the calm Pacific Ocean, the Coronado Islands (which lay offshore in Mexican waters), Point Loma and the entrance to beautiful San Diego Bay, the mountains behind San Diego and southeast to the quiet Glorietta Bay. What could be a more picturesque setting for a world-class resort?

On January 12, 1887, a ground-breaking ceremony for the new hotel was held. Isabel Babcock turned the first shovel of dirt. (In 1938, James Reid recalled the ceremony as having taken place in March, but according to newspaper

accounts in the San Diego *Union* , the ground-breaking was in January and the laying of the foundation was in March.)

Materials and labor were scarce in San Diego at the time. A large contingent of unskilled Chinese laborers, along with master carpenters, plumbers and other craftsmen, were transported by boat from San Francisco and Oakland in order to work on the giant project. Anxious to complete the hotel as soon as possible, Babcock and his designers would have liked workers for day and night shifts, but finding workers for the day shift proved difficult enough. According to newspaper accounts, the labor union saw to it that its workers were on the job for only nine hours per day. To compensate, the unskilled Chinese laborers were trained on the job. Eventually, enough workers were found to man the construction site twenty-four hours per day.

Bricks were fired from a kiln, built nearby specifically for the construction project, and the San Diego Granite Company provided rock from quarries in Temecula Canyon.

When work began on the twelve-foot-high foundation in March, 1887, some 100 barrels of cement were poured daily.

In the meantime, china was ordered from Paris, glassware from Belgium, toilet seats from England and 21,000 yards of carpet were shipped from Lowell, Massachusetts. A Boston furniture maker designed and produced wooden chairs, christened "Coronado Diners."

Construction could not proceed fast enough. As the foundation went up, so did expectations and it was announced prematurely that the huge hotel would be ready by November. In September, a Mr. and Mrs. H.B. Wilkins made the hotel's first room reservations, actually selecting their room from the architects' plans. By October, a twenty-foot flag of blue silk was unfurled. However, it was soon obvious that construction would not meet the November target date. The opening was postponed until mid-December.

At the same time he was designing and building The Del, as the Hotel del Coronado has affectionately come to be known, James Reid was working on another hotel project in the infant community. The "Josephine," a smaller wooden

structure, would actually be finished ahead of the "big hotel." This was fortunate for some of the guests of the big hotel, because when they arrived in mid-December, expecting to occupy their rooms in America's largest Pacific Coast resort, they found workmen scurrying to complete the project. Although the Josephine has long since been razed, it opened in the fall of 1887. No doubt it accommodated a good many disappointed guests who had traveled thousands of miles to be among the first to experience the dream resort by the sea.

The Josephine, which was later renamed the "Iturbitide," was built in the same Queen Anne style as its counterpart on the beach. It had a tall tower, and a shingled cupola and similar wood turnings. Like the Hotel del Coronado, the Josephine had electricity, receiving power from Babcock's new power plant on The Del property. (The power plant structure, complete with smokestack, can be seen today along the east driveway entrance to the resort. It serves as the advertising and communications office for the hotel.)

Furniture started arriving at the hotel's unfinished structure in November, 1887, followed, in December, by the first members of the staff. Because the project was behind schedule, pressures mounted for the hotel's first manager, John B. Seghers, who was also called upon to act as the hotel's first decorator!

The San Diego *Union* recorded an "informal" opening of the hotel on February 1, 1888, with the promise of a "formal" opening in the near future. At this time, the Nelson Morris party from Chicago moved en suite into rooms 138 and 141, and became the first official guests to put their names in the hotel's register. In the following days, they were joined by guests from across the nation, including those from Kansas City, St. Louis, San Francisco, Minneapolis, Cheyenne, Omaha, Boston, Washington, D.C. and New York City.

On February 19, the hotel served its first meals; this was some three weeks after the first guests had checked in. Construction continued for the next several months. However, the inconvenience didn't stop people from flocking to this unusual Victorian seaside resort which mirrored those of Brighton along the southern English coastline.

(Above): John D. Spreckels built the pier pictured above in the early 1900s.

(Below): Early hotel laundry delivery vehicle. The Hotel del Coronado has always had its own laundry facilities. Today, in addition to providing service to the hotel, it also services some twenty nearby hotels and motels.

(Opposite): Early woodworking tools used in the hotel's construction.

In the early 1890s, the hotel's sun porches also served as entry ways to rooms as there were no hallways as they exist today.

Those first meals were served in what was simply called "the dining room" (now known as the Crown Room), and it is one of America's monumental architectural achievements. Stretching 156 feet long, sixty-six feet wide and rising thirty-three feet high, the magnificent sugar pine-paneled ceiling was hand-fitted without a single nail. It remains one of the nation's largest pillar-free rooms.

The U.S. economy had been strong when construction began in 1887, but it soured and fell on hard times as the hotel neared completion; this probably explains the delay of the grand opening. The economic downturn sent people away from San Diego—and back to their homes—as quickly as they had come.

As Babcock and Story were realizing their dream, yet another vision had begun to take shape. John D. Spreckels sailed into the quiet San Diego harbor in July of 1887. The son of "sugar king" Claus Spreckels (he imported sugar from Hawaii to San Francisco), John was determined to make his own mark in the world. He quickly fell in love with the sleepy port in spite, or perhaps because, of its many needs. One of his first ventures was to build a coal bunker and a wharf that would service the area's railroad trains. He thus assured their valuable continued presence.

Over the next forty years, Spreckels would join San Diego's other pioneers, such as Alonzo Horton, Babcock, and Story, in helping to create a modern city. By far, Spreckels was the wealthiest of them all. He built a streetcar system, bought and published the two leading newspapers, the *Union* and the *Tribune*, developed real estate, became a banker, brought in much-needed water from the mountains and, in a project that nearly ruined him financially, Spreckels built the San Diego, Arizona and Eastern Railway. This system went around and through the steep mountains east of the city and linked the desert and mountain communities to San Diego.

Almost from his first day in San Diego, Spreckels was intrigued by the development of Coronado and by the fascinating structure which dominated the horizon of the flat land across the bay. Babcock, who had run into financial difficulties, successfully convinced Spreckels to invest in the Coronado Beach Company. As the years passed, Spreckels' investment grew. By the turn of the

(Opposite top): Construction was begun in March, 1887, and the hotel opened just eleven months later!

(Opposite bottom): J. D. Spreckels as a young man.

(Left): The U.S. Navy began using the beaches near the Hotel del Coronado to train in the early 1900s, during the days of the Great White Fleet. Today, the nearby Naval installations still use the beach areas near the famed resort for physical fitness and swim training.

(Below): Heavyweight champion Jack Dempsey was a frequent visitor to the Hotel.

(Bottom): Among the famous heroes visiting The Del was baseball great Babe Ruth (on left).

century, Spreckels was running the company and hotel from his home in San Francisco; Babcock had become just another employee on the payroll.

Prior to the arrival of the Spreckels family at the hotel in 1906, The Del was closed from June until December of 1902, for renovation and completion of some unfinished work. It was during this time that the famed Tent City emerged to the south along the Silver Strand.

Much of Coronado's social life centered around Tent City, according to hotel historian Stephen S. Oakford. It had the beach, boating activities and an indoor salt water plunge. It offered concerts, plays and vaudeville shows. Local residents as well as hotel guests flocked to these performances. Tent City flourished as one of the country's most popular vacation spots until, sadly, it closed in 1939.

The San Francisco earthquake of 1906 was all it took to convince Spreckels to make San Diego his permanent home. He loaded his family and belongings aboard his yacht, *Lurline,* and brought them south to the Hotel del Coronado. They would live at the hotel until their splendid granite mansion was built across the street. (This mansion can be seen today as the Glorietta Bay Inn.)

Spreckels guided the hotel through one of its most opulent periods. During this era, The Del was visited by several U.S. presidents. In 1909, it hosted San Diego's first Charity Ball. And the most famous state visit of all, that of His Royal Highness, the Prince of Wales, took place in 1920.

When Spreckels died in 1927, his successors faced serious problems. There were matters of succession within the companies that controlled his holdings. (He had invested heavily in a decaying streetcar system; the once-popular public transportation system was gradually being replaced by the private automobile.)

In later years, when the Great Depression hit, the Spreckels family sold some properties, held onto others. The Hotel del Coronado was kept in the portfolio. It did not officially go up for sale until after World War II. The years had taken their toll, and The Del was no longer the well-polished resort it had once been. The grand visits of Eastern and Hollywood elite had all but ceased, while the hotel was burdened by some 100 permanent guests who lived in it on the American Plan (meals included) at a low rate.

(Above):The first of many presidents to visit The Del–Benjamin Harrison, 1891.

(Below):An exciting event at The Del ballroom, 1924.

(Opposite): An early photograph of the Hotel del Coronado.

Egyptian Ball to Be Gorgeous

Miss Dorothy Shea of Portland, Ore., and Miss Margaret P. Elkins of Los Angeles. Both girls will be featured in the Egyptian Ball at Hotel del Coronado.

A strange and little-known transaction took place in 1948, which conveyed ownership of the Hotel del Coronado to Robert A. Nordblom and a small group of investors. However, prominent Kansas City hotelier Barney Goodman became the hotel's fourth owner only two days later.

Goodman had the vision and the business sense to begin restoring the old hotel to the prominence it previously enjoyed. The permanent guests were asked to leave, a fifth floor was added along with another fifty rooms. Goodman renovated existing rooms and improved both the outward and inward appearance with much-needed paint.

Unfortunately, Goodman's untimely death in 1951 curtailed the hotel's complete renovation. The hotel was held in trust for his two sons until 1960, but the impetus for renovation died with Goodman.

San Diego businessman John S. Alessio became the hotel's fifth owner in 1960. Alessio immediately set upon a new renovation and improvement program. Public areas and guest rooms were his targets as he spent millions of dollars on the project. It was Alessio who had the Grand Ballroom's high ceiling lowered to allow for better sound control. The original narrow windows of the Crown and Coronet rooms were removed and replaced with the huge plate glass windows of today.

The Hotel del Coronado Corporation purchased the hotel from Alessio in 1963, again, before renovation was fully realized. M. Larry Lawrence, the sixth owner, has restored the hotel to its original Victorian splendor and charm, while retaining its attraction as a pleasure spot and as a scene for San Diego social events. Lawrence has also expanded the hotel's appeal as a resort and convention center.

A continuous renovation program was instituted by Lawrence's design team. Its "Perfect Rooms Program" ensures that guest rooms are kept in perfect condition. A crew of six works its way around the hotel every four months doing painting, wallpapering, electrical, plumbing, and carpentry upgrades as needed.

M. LARRY LAWRENCE

One of Southern California's most successful developers and entrepreneurs is Chicago-born M. Larry Lawrence. After serving in World War II as a merchant marine, Lawrence attended the University of Arizona where he became a football hero. He returned to his native Chicago after college and entered several different professions: he was a partner in a public relations firm, an active real estate broker, a general contractor and an insurance broker. During this period, in the 1940s and early 1950s, he developed more than $60 million in construction projects.

He moved his family to California in 1953. There he continued his general contracting and insurance businesses and added securities to his list of activities. Since moving to California, he has been responsible for more than $300 million in residential and commercial projects.

He is noted for his wide range of philanthropic projects as well as for a variety of civic works. Lawrence is well known on a national scale for his political activities. He has also served as a member of the Federal Home Loan Bank board.

His first love, however, is his grand lady by the Pacific—the Hotel del Coronado—which he has guided carefully through a period of renaissance since 1963. As Chairman of the Board of the Hotel del Coronado Corporation, he faced some tough decisions over the years; the first was whether or not to invest millions of dollars in order to bring The Del back to her original state of elegance and beauty.

"I felt we would have to do some serious renovation to justify the hotel's continued existence," he said in an interview. As a developer, his experience with architecture and engineering dictated quite clearly what had to be done to make the hotel functional. When his organization took control of the hotel, its mechanical and electrical elements didn't work. The plumbing was in such bad shape that little, if any, water pressure went beyond the third floor, and in some areas, there was no water at all. Other areas simply had no hot water. It was clear to Lawrence that all these matters had to be rectified immediately or authorities would certainly condemn portions of and possibly the entire hotel, thereby forcing its closure.

Between 1963 and 1988, $80 million was spent restoring, repairing and replacing those systems least noticed by the public. Mechanical, plumbing, electrical, heating, ventilation, and cooking gas lines were improved and a myriad of structural changes were made just to keep the hotel alive.

Lawrence was concerned with fire and safety codes. Measures were taken that exceeded the requirements, giving the Hotel del Coronado one of the best fire ratings of any building in the world. This is a point of special pride to Lawrence because The Del is one of the world's largest wooden structures. The hotel's Grinnell sprinkler system is one of the finest, most expensive of its kind and provides guests the utmost in fire safety. "You'll float away before you even smell smoke," quips Lawrence.

Lawrence correctly gambled on making the Hotel del Coronado one of Southern California's largest and most successful meeting and convention facilities. He constructed the Grande Hall with a meeting capacity of 1500, thereby increasing the hotel's ability to accommodate large groups. The hotel has expanded from 399 to 700 rooms due to the addition of the seven-floor Ocean Towers complex and the poolside complex.

But the new facilities were not created at the expense of the Reid Brothers' fragile architecture of nearly a century ago. Lawrence brought in the best designers so the newer complexes blended skillfully and beautifully with the main building, maintaining the hotel's familiar white body and bright red roof trademark.

Lawrence is highly respected for his self-made financial success, but no accomplishment is more dear to him than his restoration of one of the world's most beautiful man-made historic landmarks—the grandame of American seaside resorts—the Hotel del Coronado.

THE HOTEL DEL CORONADO'S M. LARRY LAWRENCE & SHELIA DAVIS LAWRENCE RECEIVE UNITED STATES GOVERNMENT APPOINTMENTS TO SWITZERLAND

Left to right: Shelia Davis Lawrence, U.S. Representative to the World Conservation Union; M. Larry Lawrence, U.S. Ambassador to Switzerland; Deputy-Chief of Protocol Fred Duvall; and Vice-President Al Gore.

In March 1994, the United States Senate voted overwhelmingly to confirm the Hotel del Coronado's own Larry Lawrence as Ambassador to Switzerland.

Nominated by President Clinton for this position, Mr. Lawrence, one of the most respected entrepreneurs in the United States, takes his many years of business, political and financial experience to this position.

Mr. Lawrence, a lifelong member of the Democratic Party, was one of the first to receive an invitation by then President-Elect Bill Clinton to the initial Economic Summit in Little Rock, Arkansas. Along with board chairmen from many of the country's leading industries, as well as invited economic scholars, Mr. Lawrence gave his suggestions and solutions to alleviate the economic slowdown that the United States was then suffering. Mr. Lawrence is also an active supporter of NAFTA which he feels will create more quality jobs for many California residents.

Shelia Davis Lawrence was appointed as a Special United States Representative to the IUCN—The World Conservation Union, an international organization whose primary focus is world-wide environmental conservation.

Mrs. Lawrence, also a very active member of the Democratic Party, spearheaded the Southern California effort to elect Bill Clinton, and under her guidance the Democratic Party scored one of its greatest California victories in recent history.

STARSTRUCK

AT THE DEL

Over the years, more celebrities of the arts, entertainment and sports worlds have visited the Hotel del Coronado than any other resort in North America. Add to this the countless local celebrations and you have one of the world's truly great places where the famous relax and hide from or mingle with everyday travelers. And they do it amid the luxury and elegance that was once the style and grace of Europe's elite.

Countless tales exist—some true, some legendary and some nearly forgotten—of the notables who have experienced The Del. One such story is recalled by Carleton Lichty, former vice-chairman of the corporate board.

"Jimmy Doolittle, the famed Army aviator, told this story on himself," recalls Lichty. "General Doolittle and his wife lived in a little house in Coronado during the 1920s when Doolittle was a second lieutenant stationed at Rockwell Field (now known as North Island Naval Air Station). The Doolittles dreamed of staying at The Del. They saved their money and finally had enough to check in and enjoy the honeymoon they never had. The problem was, according to the general, they didn't have enough money to buy food at the hotel, or so they thought. They ate at a greasy spoon restaurant some blocks away from the hotel, and it wasn't until they checked out that the couple discovered the hotel was on the American Plan, meaning that meals were included in the price of the room."

Lichty, one of the nation's most respected hoteliers, was in charge of managing The Del on two different occasions, first during John Alessio's tenure as owner, and then returning in 1965 for present owner Larry Lawrence. Like managers before him, Lichty saw his share of celebrities, presidents and foreign dignitaries. The largest state dinner held outside of Washington, D.C., was held at the hotel in 1970, when President Richard Nixon hosted Mexican President Gustavo Diaz Ordaz in the Crown Room, site of many other spectacular dinners over the years.

President Nixon selected the Hotel del Coronado because of his strong interest in history, and because he knew there was no dining room in America that equaled the Crown Room in scale, aesthetic beauty and social grace. It was an ideal setting

(Opposite): Marilyn Monroe greeted her fans during the 1958 filming of Some Like It Hot.

Celebrities and the politically lofty frequent the Hotel del Coronado. President Ronald Reagan (below) hosted a mini-conference at the hotel in 1982. President George Bush (right) talking tennis with Hotel Del resident tennis pro Ben Press. Tennis Star Chris Evert (below, middle), playing on one of The Del's championship courts. The TV series, "Hart to Hart" (bottom), taping a segment at The Del in 1983.

for the pomp and ceremony Nixon felt was necessary for his Mexican counterpart. For San Diegans, it was a once-in-a-lifetime pageant, a chance to indulge personally in the sort of elaborate state ceremony which citizens outside Washington, D.C., rarely have the opportunity to see. More than 1000 invited guests attended the gala dinner, including former President Lyndon B. Johnson and his wife Lady Bird, Secretary of State William Rogers, Attorney General John Mitchell, General of the Army Omar Bradley, California Governor Ronald Reagan and his wife Nancy, presidential aides Henry Kissinger, H. R. Haldeman, Ronald Ziegler, and seven U.S. senators, including Arizona's Barry Goldwater. And the event was not limited to politicians: John Wayne headed an all-star Hollywood cast that included Frank Sinatra, Art Linkletter, Red Skelton and Cesar Romero. Lichty recalls the evening as "one of the most dramatic and elegant in all the rich history of the Hotel del Coronado."

Over the years, The Del has hosted fourteen U.S. presidents, beginning with Benjamin Harrison in April, 1891. In the years to follow, the hotel would welcome presidents including William McKinley, William Howard Taft, Woodrow Wilson, Franklin D. Roosevelt (who visited on a number of occasions before and during his presidency), Dwight D. Eisenhower, John F. Kennedy, Richard M. Nixon, Jimmy Carter, Ronald Reagan (in October of 1982, President Reagan hosted a mini-summit conference for Mexican President Miguel de la Madrid in suite 3253, now called the "Summit Suite" in honor of the occasion), George Bush, and most recently President Bill Clinton.

President Reagan is no stranger to The Del, which was one of his favorite retreats while he was an actor, then as governor of California and later as president. Suite 3119, the largest in the Victorian Building, was named the "Governor's Suite" in his honor. President Clinton visited The Del twice during his presidential campaign, returning as president the following spring for a family vacation.

According to the San Diego *Union*, less auspicious political guests have also stayed at The Del: Vice President Stevenson in 1893, the widow of John Jay Knox in 1895, Robert Todd Lincoln, son of the late president, in 1896 and Montgomery Ward in 1900.

THE HOTEL DEL CORONADO CELEBRATES A TRADITION OF PRESIDENTIAL VISITS.

The world-renowned Hotel del Coronado has played gracious host to 14 United States Presidents since opening in 1888. The initial Presidential visit occurred in 1891 when President Benjamin Harrison arrived at the Del. In May 1993, President William Jefferson Clinton stayed at the Del while delivering his economic message to the residents of Southern California.

William Jefferson Clinton

Ronald Reagan

Jimmy Carter

George Bush

Gerald Ford

Lyndon B. Johnson

John F. Kennedy

Richard Nixon

Dwight D. Eisenhower

Franklin Delano Roosevelt

Woodrow Wilson

William Howard Taft

William McKinley

Benjamin Harrison

PLURIBUS UNUM

(Left): Ramon Navarro and Anita Page in a scene from The Flying Fleet, which was the first of many movies to be filmed in full or in part at The Del.

(Right): Margarita Fisher, actress of the silent screen and San Diego girl. Married to Harry Pollard, director of Pollard Film Play Company, she starred in Pearl of Paradise (1915), thought to have been shot at the Lubin Studios in Coronado.

L. Frank Baum's fabled Land of Oz bears a striking resemblance to The Del's well known conical spires. Baum visited the hotel many times in the early 1900s and eventually settled in Coronado.

During the hotel's construction in 1887, the world's most famous inventor, who had more than 1000 patents in his name when he died, personally supervised the installation of his incandescent lighting system. Thomas Alva Edison returned to the hotel in 1904, to throw the switch on The Del's first Christmas tree, a star pine which still stands on the front lawn at the east end of the Crown Room. Edison again returned to San Diego in 1915, for the Pan-American Exposition. This time he arrived with good friends Harvey Firestone and Henry Ford. They came at the invitation of G. Aubrey Davidson, who made The Del his permanent home.

World famous New York publisher John Pulitzer made headlines along the California coast because he was among The Del's first guests when it opened in February, 1888. Charles Nordhoff, a popular political writer of the day, was a guest in December, 1890. (His grandson, Charles Nordhoff, co-authored the best-selling classic, *Mutiny on the Bounty*, in later years.)

Over the years, writers have been attracted to The Del. The hotel has charm and elegance, and maintains a mystique that fires the imagination; no doubt these characteristics have inspired a great many literary efforts. L. Frank Baum wrote books for his Wizard of Oz series at the hotel. His first visits were as a glassware salesman, later as a writer of these children's stories. He and his wife spent a month at a time at The Del, simply ingesting the peaceful setting which inspired him to design the chandeliers now hanging from the Crown Room restaurant ceiling. Illustrations in the Oz books show a marked similarity between his architectural fantasies and the hotel, and movie watchers may note the Emerald City castle in the film version of *The Wizard of Oz* was also based on The Del's Victorian style. And, author Henry James managed to work in a two-day stay at the hotel in 1905, while traveling from his home in the East to a speaking engagement in Los Angeles.

Hollywood first discovered The Del in 1927, when it was selected as a location site for the Metro-Goldwyn-Mayer silent production of *The Flying Fleet*, which starred Ramon Navarro and a beautiful young actress named Anita Page. (A young and talented actress, Miss Page later starred in *Broadway Melody*, the

(Above): Edward, Prince of Wales at a reception dinner in his honor, 1920. From left to right: Mrs. J. E. Kuhne, Governor William Stevens, Ellis Spreckels, the Prince of Wales, Mrs. Wilde (wife of mayor of San Diego). What were the prince and Ellis Spreckels discussing so intently? According to social columnist Eileen Jackson, "Hollywood, the movies, and all the glamour gals of those days."

CLOVER CLUB COCKTAIL

As described earlier, the royal visit by Britain's Prince of Wales in 1920, was a memorable one; people are still talking about it. A small episode, when the prince unexpectedly walked from the hotel to the nearby home of Claus Spreckels at 1043 Ocean Boulevard, resulted in the documentation of a tasty cocktail that was served to the prince. Ellis Spreckels, owner John Spreckels' daughter-in-law, had played an important part in arranging the royal visit. The prince wanted to personally pay his respects and thank her for all of her hard work. When he arrived, Mrs. Spreckels was just returning from the beach with her children and was naturally caught by surprise. After quickly getting out of her beach attire, the hostess and her daughters came downstairs to greet the royal visitor. There, Mrs. Spreckels served what she called the "Clover Club Cocktail."

The recipe for this royal concoction is as follows:

Juice from 1 lemon	2 tsp of grenadine
White of 1 egg	1 jigger of dry gin

Blend over cracked ice and strain.

first musical to win an Academy Award for Best Picture.) Miss Page adopted Coronado as her Shangri-la. After retiring, at the age of 26, she married a U.S. Naval officer and lived within a mile of the hotel.

During the 1920s and 1930s, The Del attracted many other Hollywood celebrities. Some of the more glamorous names included Mary Pickford, Tallulah Bankhead and Greta Garbo. Mae West was a guest in 1934. Charlie Chaplin was a regular member of Coronado's polo crowd which made the hotel its headquarters. And Sarah Bernhardt, the grand lady of American theater, found the hotel "charmante."

When movie companies come to the San Diego area, more often than not they select the Hotel del Coronado as their prime location site. In 1972, the hotel became the background for "Ghost Story," a television series starring the late Sebastian Cabot. It didn't fare well in the ratings and was soon dropped by the network. Nevertheless, the Victorian architecture of The Del served well to create the required atmosphere. Other movies made over the years include *Loving Couples*, with Shirley MacLaine, *Wicked, Wicked*, a forgettable horror story, and *$*, with Goldie Hawn. Television movies filmed in part at the hotel have included: *The Girl, the Gold Watch and Everything*; *Captains and Kings*; and *Rich Man, Poor Man*. Television series such as "Hart to Hart," with Robert Wagner, and "Simon & Simon," with Jamieson Parker and Gerald McRaney, "Lifestyles of the Rich and Famous" and countless television commercials, have also used The Del.

The Del was also the subject of a popular Hollywood film. In 1975, Richard Matheson, who worked with Rod Serling on the popular "Twilight Zone" series, wrote a novel titled *Bid Time Return*. It is an enchanting story that takes the protagonist back through time to 1896; it is set entirely at the Hotel del Coronado. The book was made into a motion picture titled *Somewhere in Time*.

(Opposite): Children practicing diving at Tent City, c. 1920. Tent City was the center of many Coronado social activities until its closure in 1939.

Esther Williams and her sons were frequent guests in the 1950s (top left). They returned for the 1988 Centennial Celebration (top right).

(Below): Interior of bathhouse, 1890. The building, located a few blocks east of the hotel, served numerous bathers until it was demolished around 1930.

(Above): Stars attended a gala and exchanged awards on the 25th anniversary, in 1984, of filming the movie **Some Like It Hot**. From left, director Billy Wilder, Jack Lemmon and Tony Curtis.

(Opposite): Marilyn Monroe and Jack Lemmon, on location at The Hotel del Coronado for the 1958 filming of **Some Like It Hot,** stroll, in costume, along the beach.

(Below): Marilyn Monroe sizzles with **Some Like It Hot** co-star Tony Curtis.

The list of movies made at the Hotel del Coronado is a long one. But *Some Like It Hot* elicits the warmest and most affectionate smiles from the faces of long-time staff members. Filmed in part at the resort in 1958, it starred Marilyn Monroe, Jack Lemmon and Tony Curtis and was directed by Billy Wilder. Over the years, the film has gathered a cult following among movie aficionados. Many regard it as Academy Award-winning producer-director Billy Wilder's most successful comedy, as well as Marilyn Monroe's finest performance. Hotel staffers who worked at The Del during the filming recall Monroe as she romped through the hotel halls and played on the beach with Lemmon, Curtis and co-stars George Raft, Joe E. Brown and Pat O'Brien.

The movie is fondly embraced by the management of The Del and the neighboring Coronado and San Diego communities. In fact, a special twenty-fifth anniversary celebration, which honored Lemmon and Curtis and paid special tribute to Wilder, was held in the Grand Ballroom on April 28, 1984. Several hundred citizens, including Hollywood celebrities and a host of international media members, attended the gala event which marked the importance of the Hotel del Coronado as a motion picture location site and as a center of social activity.

Another full-length feature film shot at The Del was *The Stunt Man,* starring Peter O'Toole. For those who saw the movie, no, the hotel was not damaged in the least…a tower explodes in the film, but in reality, it was only a model!

By far, the most talked-about celebrity guest in the Hotel del Coronado's more than 100 years of existence was His Royal Highness the Prince of Wales. He later became King Edward VIII of England, only to abdicate his throne before his coronation for "the woman I love!" The woman he loved was a former Coronado housewife who lived within blocks of The Del. She was the wife of the commanding officer of the nearby North Island Naval Air Station at the time of the prince's visit in April, 1920. (The port of San Diego was a stop on his around-the-world cruise aboard the *HMS Renown.*)

Ever since the royal visit, it has been hotly argued as to whether or not Wallis Warfield Spencer met the prince at the Hotel del Coronado. The occasion was a full fifteen years prior to their "official" introduction in England, when she was married to a Baltimore businessman and living in London. But there is evi-

(Right): Tennis greats of the early 1900s, such as the Sutton sisters (Miss May Sutton depicted), Maurice McLaughlin and Tom Bundy, played on the first lawn tennis courts located across the street from The Del.

(Below): Beginning in 1899, the golf course, as described in the hotel brochure, consisted of "a circular course of nine holes extending over a rolling tract of land. The total distance is 2730 yards. Bunkers and hazards are properly arranged so that the skill of the veteran golfer undergoers a severe test in making the round." By 1900, it had eighteen holes and was 5318 yards in length. Putting greens were 120 feet in diameter, made of asphalt and covered with a thin coat of sand to make them "fast or slow as desired." In 1959, the course was moved to its current site.

(Opposite): Today, the Hotel del Coronado has six lighted championship tennis courts overlooking the blue Pacific. Celebrities and famed professional players frequent these courts.

dence the two may have at least had a face-to-face exchange of pleasantries at the huge gala in the hotel's Grand Ballroom (in which more than 1000 people jammed to see the world's most eligible bachelor), or the next day aboard the *HMS Renown* where the prince hosted a tea for the wives of senior U.S. Naval officers. Most likely, Mrs. Spencer met the prince in the receiving line in the Ballroom. (On another evening, a state dinner was hosted for the prince by San Diego Mayor Louis Wilde in the hotel's Crown Room. California Governor W. D. Stevens attended, along with eighty carefully selected guests; there is no evidence Commander Spencer and his wife were invited.) There are unsubstantiated reports that Commander Spencer was out of town—transferred to a new duty assignment. If these reports are true, it is highly unlikely Mrs. Spencer would have attended without an escort. The legend persists that, indeed, the future Duke and Duchess of Windsor met each other for the first time at the Hotel del Coronado—but nobody except the two principals will ever know the details.

Today, there are several reminders of the famous visitor and the mark he left on this grandame of the Pacific. The hotel's gourmet restaurant, the Prince of Wales Restaurant, is named in his honor. The Duke, years later, wrote a letter to the hotel management, complimenting the restaurant's menu and thanking the hotel for the kind remembrance; he experienced few kindnesses after leaving England in 1936. The only known photograph of the prince in the Crown Room was taken during the state dinner. In it, he is seated beside a young woman; the two are deeply engrossed in conversation. The woman was Ellis Spreckels, daughter-in-law of the hotel's owner, John D. Spreckels. A world traveler and a popular socialite in the Coronado and San Diego communities, Mrs. Spreckels later was asked the details of her conversation with the prince. "He was mainly interested in Hollywood and the stars," she replied.

In fact, Ellis Spreckels went to London some years later to counsel Mrs. Spencer, her long-time Coronado friend, who was pondering whether or not to marry the British monarch. Mrs. Spreckels' advice is not known, but the world well knows of Mrs. Spencer's final decision.

Less well-known was the April, 1898, visit by Belgium's heir apparent, Prince Albert. According to newspaper reports, Prince Albert registered at the

A hunting party typical of those organized by the Hotel del Coronado in the 1890s. The stained glass window in the upper right hand corner depicts the mythical Amazon leader, Califia (for whom California was named).

(Left): Since the 1890s, The Del has been California's premier oceanfront resort.

(Opposite): The Hotel del Coronado overlooks the picturesque Glorietta Bay as well as the Coronado Golf Course.

Cesar Romero and Anne Jeffreys were among the celebrities at the Hotel del Coronado's $3 million Centennial celebration in February of 1988.

Owner M. Larry Lawrence welcomed entertainer Phyllis Diller to the Centennial Gala.

hotel under an American alias. The San Diego *Union* reporter who uncovered the disguise described the prince as "unpretentious and sensible." These words were meant as a compliment, considering those days of England's Queen Victoria and Europe's royalty.

The Prince of Wales' visit in 1920 created much pomp, ceremony and notoriety. But The Del's first royal visitor was Hawaii's last monarch, King Kalakaua. He came for the Christmas holidays in the 1890s. This popular royal visitor entertained U.S. Army and Naval officers in the parlor adjacent to his suite.

The Del's first recorded social function was in December, 1887, prior to its official opening. The event was a dance held by the management for the staff members who had just come from the East. In those early days, when the hotel first opened, informal dances were a regular occurrence, as were Sunday afternoon band concerts performed by the hotel's own band.

The first meal ever served at the hotel was prepared by Chef M. Frederick Compagnon on December 27, 1887—again, before the official opening—in the Garden Patio. This inaugural meal was enjoyed by the hotel's first manager, J.B. Seghers, his wife, and a party of twenty intimate friends, including owners Elisha Babcock and H.L. Story, and architect James Reid. Today, the Hotel del Coronado has four popular restaurants which serve a wide variety of dishes. These restaurants are favorites with hotel guests and also with the greater San Diego community.

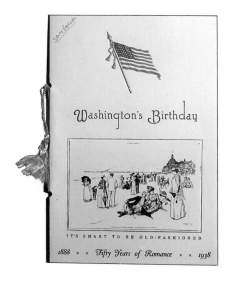

The Hotel del Coronado has been the site of countless social functions over the years. But one of its greatest honors is hosting the annual Charity Ball, one of San Diego's oldest traditions. The Ball began as a benefit for San Diego children in 1909, and is still held at the hotel each year to benefit the Children's Hospital and Health Center. It is regarded as one of San Diego's most prestigious social functions. Other popular social events held at The Del include the Mardi Gras for the Junior of Social Service, the La Jolla Debutante Ball, and the San Diego Chamber of Commerce's annual Flag and General Officers Ball (which brings together high-ranking military and civilian leaders).

The Del has witnessed San Diego's rich military history, from the days of the 1890s, to Glenn Curtiss' first amphibious landing on Coronado, to the mammoth Naval and Marine buildup during World War II. Through the years, as San Diego grew to be one of the nation's foremost military communities, The Del grew to be an important social center for Naval and Marine officers. Eileen Jackson, a long-time San Diego *Tribune* social columnist who covered San Diego and Coronado for over forty years, pointed out, "They've always liked the Navy in Coronado. I can recall people saying they enjoy the Navy folks because they are not so provincial; they're well-traveled." Jackson feels the civilian community, like its military neighbors, are also well-traveled and are certainly not provincial.

The British were frequent visitors to the San Diego Naval facilities. The Del served as a favorite entertainment and relaxation haunt because of its English flavor, and also because of its nearby polo facility. This gave our American officers the opportunity to challenge their cousins to polo matches. Eyewitness reports reveal that—somehow—the British didn't get the best horses and oddly enough, our American hosts maintained a certain equestrian advantage during these contests!

Sports of all kinds have attracted visitors to The Del. The huge billiard room used to be the main attraction in the lower portion of the hotel. A bowling alley was also a popular venue, as were yachting and fishing off Coronado's coast.

Today, the Hotel del Coronado is a popular beach and tennis facility. It has one of the most beautiful expanses of sandy beach anywhere in the country and its six lighted tennis courts regularly attract professional players (such as Chris Evert) as well as amateur player-guests.

In the early days, the hotel—and its many recreational amenities—attracted celebrities, heads-of-state, captains of industry, high-ranking military officers and the wealthy. Today, San Diego is California's second largest city and the nation's seventh, and these people can come to the Hotel del Coronado and remain relatively unnoticed. But when the hotel was young and San Diego and Coronado together had fewer than 20,000 residents, such notables were bound to—and indeed did—make headlines!

Mary Martin joined George Burns at the grand Centennial Celebration.

Tony Curtis, who starred in Some Like It Hot *with Marilyn Monroe at The Del, escorts Ruta Lee (left) and Debbie Reynolds (right) at the centennial celebration.*

The centennial celebration program was unveiled to the world on March 19, 1987, when a festive party was held for 500 guests at the hotel. Hostesses in historical costumes (top) greeted attendees in the Centennial Pavilion.

The Hotel del Coronado's yearlong centennial celebration has come to be known as the grandest spectacle ever witnessed since this Victorian masterpiece opened on February 19, 1888. It was only fitting that the culmination of a full century as the Pacific Coast's grandame be heralded with unrivaled fanfare and a yearlong program of events, including a Centennial Gala unequaled in its elegance, performances by some of the nation's top entertainers and exquisite cuisine.

Although a yearlong celebration was planned well in advance of 1988, the crowning point of the anniversary unquestionably was the Centennial Gala of February 19, 20 and 21. A centennial committee was formed to ensure that this weekend would be remembered as the grandest in the hotel's history. One of the world's top party coordinators, Wendy Moss of "An Affair to Remember," planned the Centennial Gala weekend. Among other tasks, her crew spent months working on outfitting the hotel for the centennial celebration, ensuring that one of the world's largest dining rooms, the Crown Room, was made to look more elegant than ever before. Lighting crews and fabric companies teamed up to give this National Historic Landmark restaurant, indeed the entire hotel, a new "look" in keeping with tradition but with a fresh eye toward the future.

The weekend began with the largest and most extraordinary party ever held at the hotel. Visitors on Friday, February 19, were treated to a party that encompassed the entire hotel! A "Some Like It Hot" speakeasy, a Wizard of Oz Emerald City replica, a '50s diner—all were recreated through the use of amazing sets and accomplished actors portraying the hotel's most famous guests (Marilyn Monroe, Thomas Edison, Prince of Wales, etc.).

Saturday began with a gorgeous breakfast buffet, followed by a celebrity-filled tennis tournament and a harbor cruise. Gaming tables were worked around the clock in between time. That evening, the actual Centennial Gala took place in the hotel.

The Food and Beverage Department of the Hotel del Coronado had been waiting for this event for years. The crew prepared a magnificent menu for the evening which was presented in the classic style that is the Hotel del Coronado trademark. After this magnificent feast, a star performance greeted the 600 guests in the Grand Ballroom, which had been redecorated by crews who had begun work directly after Friday's opening dinner. After the unforgettable Centennial Gala program, guests retired to the Gaming Room for some midnight fun, and then rested up for Sunday morning's buffet breakfast.

In between scheduled events, guests gazed at the America's Cup, prominently displayed in the hotel during the entire weekend.

The Centennial Gala was an event never to be repeated and never to be forgotten.

But there were still ten more months of celebration in store:

One of the physical changes to the hotel for the anniversary year was the addition of a 7,000 square foot Centennial Pavilion, and the new mini-museum called The History Gallery. The Pavilion was constructed next to the tennis courts at beachside, and was built in honor of the famed Coronado Tent City. In the early 1900s, it was fashionable to live in tents alongside the hotel, a tradition which lasted 37 years.

The History Gallery project was a labor of love for Centennial Coordinator Patricia Anderson, and for Linda Evans, who designed the display of historical artifacts and memorabilia. Included were some of the first light bulbs used in the electrical system supervised by Thomas Edison and many hard-to-find photographs of the early, colorful years of the hotel's history.

That historical past was evident to visitors to the hotel during its 100th anniversary through vignettes performed on a daily basis by actors recreating scenes from the hotel's past. Also every day of the centennial, a Salute to the States food presentation featured regional foods in the hotel's dining rooms.

Along with the return of ferry service to and from San Diego, and a new rubber-wheeled trolley for transporting hotel guests through town, was the restoration of The Old Oxford Hotel, Coronado's oldest public structure. The Oxford was relocated to the grounds of The Del and renovated in time for the 1988 centennial. It now houses administrative staff and has resulted in the opening of 12 new meeting rooms in the Grande Hall convention complex thanks to the relocation of staff. Guests in the front of the Ocean Towers building can see this proud structure from their rooms.

Other centennial highlights included a 10K run, various community events, special theme parties for conventions, and a January 1988 reception for media covering the Super Bowl at San Diego's Jack Murphy stadium.

No wonder Kodak picked the Hotel del Coronado as the subject of a 1988 centennial photo essay. And no wonder a Rand McNally publication stated that the Hotel del Coronado "...enjoys more fame and historical significance than perhaps any other hotel in North America." It was true during the hotel's first century and it will be true for its second.

One of the famous visitors for the 100th anniversary celebration was Snow White, who previewed the February Centennial Gala with a visit to the Centennial Pavilion (top left). Children dressed as newsboys handed out leaflets on the centennial program during the March 19 Centennial Preview party (top right).

Ten foot tall arbors adorned with 20,000 roses graced the historic Crown Room at the Centennial Gala dinner.

PERFECT IN ALL ITS
APPOINTMENTS

As it has been for nearly a century, the white wood and red shingle exterior of the Hotel del Coronado is at once spectacular and strange. Visitors usually see it for the first time from high above San Diego Harbor as they cross the massive span known as the San Diego-Coronado Bay Bridge. The hotel is a grand example of Victorian architecture and is one of the world's best preserved nineteenth century edifices.

Up close, The Del looks as if it emerged not from an architect's grand design, but from a wild fantasy. One can easily understand why this elegant wooden castle by the sea inspired L. Frank Baum to write his famous Wizard of Oz series. Upon the hotel's completion, a draftsman for the Reid Brothers architectural firm commented that "it was amazing how many rooms were built that were not even planned at the start of construction."

Everything about the Pacific Coast's largest beach resort—its shapes, lines and even its building materials—is electrifying. Unlike some forms of Victorian architecture, such as the shingle-style, or the stick-style, which are built with a simplicity of material in mind, The Del was constructed with a variety of building material: wood, shingle, glass and brick. The wood selected by the Reid Brothers was of several varieties, none of which is attractive to termites (thus answering one of the frequent questions of hotel guests). Thick planks, some of them up to fifty feet long, make up the framework of the massive Crown and Coronet Rooms, as well as the Grand Ballroom.

On the exterior of the hotel there are at least four different kinds of cedar shingles along with horizontal shiplap siding and vertical siding, both made of redwood. In addition, there are balconies with lathe-shaped ornamentation. An estimated two million red shingles make up the cover of the hotel's most striking trademark, the one-of-a-kind red roof. Elisha Babcock, the hotel's first owner, felt the red color would link the hotel to San Diego's Spanish mission heritage.

Someone once counted more than 2000 redwood doors in the main building of The Del. This same person also counted 2372 windows. Both window glass and stained glass were used in the original construction, although little of the stained glass has survived the passage of time and the hotel's many renovations.

(Above left): An Ocean Towers room. All the hotel's guest rooms were given complete makeovers and various meeting rooms were renovated at a total cost of more than $15 million during the 1987-1989 Centennial Renovation program.

(Above right): The Crown Room has been a popular dining room for guests and local residents for 100 years.

The Hotel del Coronado requires substantial maintenance. A staff of master carpenters, woodwork refinishers and painters works year-round to keep this grand wooden structure in prime condition. For example, it takes a crew of four men ten days just to polish the varnished oak wainscoting (lower panels) which encircle the Crown Room and workers lie on their backs—on scaffolding—in order to apply more than thirty gallons of polish to the ceiling.

At one time, the main building was surrounded by verandas; this was in an era when sitting outdoors in a rocking chair, enjoying the sun and ocean, was a popular pastime. Originally, the main building had 399 guest rooms and only seventy-five bathrooms. Through the years, verandas and fireplaces were removed in favor of private baths for every room.

Although the Hotel del Coronado is famous for its Victorian architecture, the hotel is actually a combination of several opulent styles associated with the reign of Britain's Queen Victoria. The Del is an outstanding example of the Queen Anne style, distinguished by its uneven design and lack of unity in everything from building materials to cupola design to window shapes.

The wood ornamentation of the exterior and interior is attributed to Charles Locke Eastlake of England, whose book, *Hints on Household Taste*, was popular in the United States during the 1870s and 1880s. Although this styling is attributed to him, it was not with his approval. Eastlake was known to be less than enamored of the Western derivation of his work.

As with any great resort, the approach and entrance is crucial. Visitors are greeted with a variety of trees and foliage. One early-day manager planted flowers in the shape of a crown on the lawn. Most photographs or drawings show traffic curling from Orange Avenue toward the ocean and coming to a halt facing Orange Avenue in front of the entrance. The traffic pattern has been altered over the years, but owner M. Larry Lawrence restored it to the way it had been in 1888. Lawrence has committed himself to restoring this grand structure to its near original state. Today's visitors arrive under a porte cochere which was designed by former hotel designer Dixon Morrow from original drawings and photographs. It was completed in 1980. The parking attendant's station is a replica of a ticket booth for the old Coronado ferry. The palm trees growing on

either side of the porte cochere are Mediterranean palms and were transported from Europe.

During the hotel's early years, there were two main entrances on the east side: men would enter through what is now the main lobby entrance while women had a separate entryway about seventy-five feet to the left (toward the ocean). The ladies used this private lobby to relax and freshen up after an arduous journey by train or dusty motorcar. Meanwhile, the men carried on with the usual check-in procedures. Although this practice would appear somewhat discriminatory today, it was actually a luxury for the ladies, who would be spared the daily attractions of the main lobby, such as fishermen displaying their catches of the day.

The hotel's beautifully-appointed foyer serves as a convenient meeting and assembly point. The U.S. Department of Interior's Historic Landmark plaque is displayed in the main foyer, as are similar proclamations from the San Diego County Board of Supervisors and the Coronado Historical Association.

Flanking the entrance to the Grand Lobby are tall ormolu sconces finished to look like gold, each with nineteen rose-colored lamps or torchiers. These sconces were manufactured in Paris during the glass lamp era and later were wired for electricity and shipped to Montreal before arriving at The Del. The Lobby is one of the Hotel del Coronado's most imposing features. Its unique design, combined with the beautifully polished Illinois oak, make it one of America's most distinctive hotel lobbies. Other than the furniture, little has changed in the Grand Lobby since 1888. It remains a wonderful example of rich English style and elegance in a most unlikely place—along the California coast near the border of Mexico!

Beside the sweeping staircase to the mezzanine level, there is the bird-cage electric elevator which has been in operation since the day the hotel opened in 1888.

In the early years, the mezzanine was known as "the gallery," a place where ladies could sit, visit or watch the lobby traffic below. "The gallery is much frequented by the ladies," proclaims a piece of early advertisement. "Thither they

(Above right): Many Victorian Building guest rooms and suites offer breathtaking views of the Pacific.

(Above left): The Hotel del Coronado has offered luxurious relaxation, complete with a sweeping view of the Pacific, since opening in 1888, as this early picture of an ocean-view lounge illustrates.

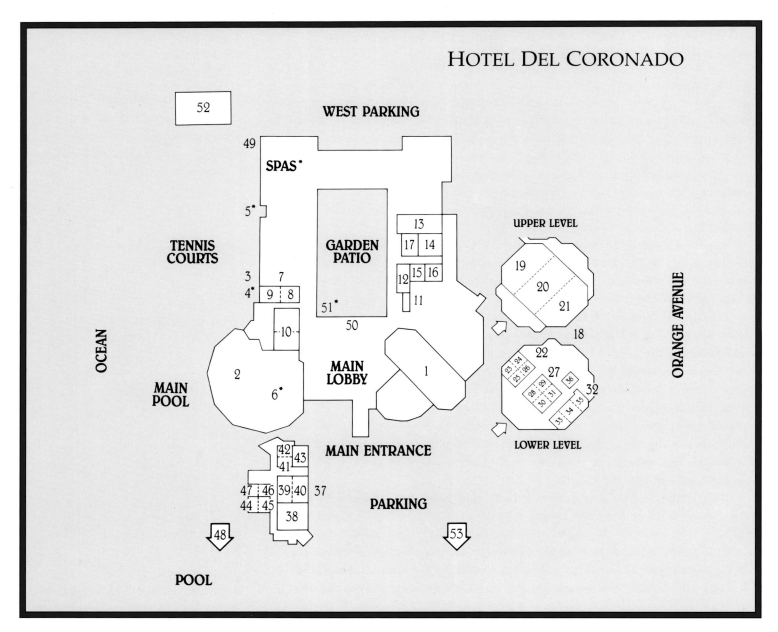

HOTEL DEL CORONADO

WEST PARKING

52

49

SPAS *

5*

TENNIS
COURTS

GARDEN
PATIO

13

17   14

UPPER LEVEL

3   7

4*   9   8

51 *

50

12 15 16

11

19

20

21

OCEAN

10

MAIN
LOBBY

2

6*

1

MAIN
POOL

18

22

23 24

25 26

27   36

28 29

30 31

32

33 34 35

LOWER LEVEL

ORANGE AVENUE

42
41 43

MAIN ENTRANCE

47 46 39 40 37

44 45

38

PARKING

48

53

POOL

(Opposite): The Hotel del Coronado's lobby has changed very little since opening in 1888 as these two photos, taken nearly 100 years apart, illustrate.

The Del's newest addition, Palm Court, left, faces on the Garden Patio and recalls the hotel's sun porches of an earlier era.

HOTEL DEL CORONADO

1 CROWN/CORONET ROOM
2 BALLROOM
3 OCEAN TERRACE
4 OCEAN TERRACE LOUNGE
5 PRINCE OF WALES
6 INTERNATIONAL ROOM
7 WINDSOR COMPLEX
8 WINDSOR ROOM
9 EMBASSY ROOM
10 CRYSTAL/CONTINENTAL ROOM
11 EXECUTIVE ROOM
12 GARDEN ROOM
13 HANOVER ROOM
14 STUART ROOM
15 YORK ROOM
16 KENT ROOM
17 TUDOR ROOM
18 GRANDE HALL
19 EMPRESS HALL
20 REGENT HALL
21 VICEROY HALL
22 BABCOCK COMPLEX
23 SALON B
24 SALON D
25 SALON A
26 SALON C
27 STORY COMPLEX
28 SALON E
29 SALON G
30 SALON F
31 SALON H
32 EDISON COMPLEX
33 SALON K
34 SALON J
35 SALON I
36 BOARD ROOM
37 POOLSIDE
38 DOVER ROOM
39 STRATFORD ROOM
40 DURHAM ROOM
41 SOMERSET ROOM
42 BRADFORD ROOM
43 MANCHESTER ROOM
44 CARDIFF ROOM
45 LANCASTER ROOM
46 PEMBROKE ROOM
47 LEEDS ROOM
48 OCEAN TOWERS
49 HALL OF HISTORY
50 PALM COURT
51 CONFERENCE REGISTRATION
52 THE COTTAGE
53 OXFORD ADMINISTRATIVE OFFICES
(*Lower Lobby Level)

resort for friendly social converse and to see newcomers entering below and registering their names."

If there is a queen of rooms it would be the Crown Room. Here, under the sugar pine ceiling which rises thirty-three feet, is one of the largest pillar-free rooms in North America. Huge state dinners for presidents, princes and heroes have been held in this room which measures 156 feet by sixty-six feet. Charles Lindbergh was feted here a few months after his historic solo flight across the Atlantic in 1927; Britain's Prince of Wales (later King Edward VIII, then Duke of Windsor) was hosted to a grand dinner in 1920; and more than 1000 guests—the largest state dinner ever held in San Diego County—were invited by President Richard Nixon as he honored Mexican President Gustavo Diaz Ordaz.

Originally, the Crown Room was the hotel's only dining room. But other facilities have since come into being and today the Crown Room is used for elegant evening dining and occasionally for breakfast and lunch when the adjacent Coronet Room cannot accommodate the demand. The Crown Room is also used for a number of special functions throughout the year: it is the scene of holiday dining on Easter, Mother's Day, Thanksgiving, Christmas and New Year's and plays host to the annual Sweetheart Dinner-Dance on Valentine's Day. The Crown Room's weekly Sunday brunch, which is served from 9 a.m. to 2 p.m., is probably the most popular dining event in all of San Diego County. A lavish display of food is placed on long tables, providing an unequaled selection of delicacies. What makes the Crown Room so spectacular is its size, its construction without visible posts or pillars, and the beautiful high-paneled ceiling placed without nails but rather with wooden pegs. In a word, the Crown Room is breathtaking!

The Coronet room, the smaller dining room adjacent to the Crown Room, measures fifty-eight feet by sixty-six feet and has a ceiling height of twenty-seven feet. Despite its intimate size (small when compared to its bigger sister), the Coronet Room has had its days of glory. Here, on October 8, 1982, President Reagan hosted Mexican President Miguel de la Madrid at a state luncheon. (The two heads of state met for a day-long summit to discuss affairs between the two

(Above): Guests from around the world flock to the hotel for its traditional holiday celebration. The Victorian Christmas tree, which stands thirty feet tall in the lobby, is the grand attraction during the hotel's annual holiday celebration. December boasts a month-long calendar of events including chorale performances, holiday teas and, of course, the tree lighting ceremony held the first week of the month.

(Preceding Pages): The Crown Room is The Del's original dining room.

(Opposite above): The hotel's Garden Patio.

(Opposite below): The newly renovated Ballroom.

nations.) The Coronet Room was originally known as the breakfast room; it is presently the hotel's primary breakfast and lunch facility but is used for evening dining when the Crown Room is engaged for a special banquet or function. Construction details and decor of this semi-circular room are essentially those of the Crown Room. The literature published when the hotel first opened remains true: the Coronet Room is where you can watch the sun rise on the eastern horizon as you have your breakfast and coffee.

Another star in the Hotel del Coronado's great public rooms is the Grand Ballroom located under the great tower on the south end of the main lobby. This magnificent room has served as a theater and a concert hall; it has also been the site of a number of gala balls over the years. In 1920, the Ball for the Prince of Wales was held in this room, and the San Diego community hosted a large reception (with more than 1000 guests) for President Jimmy Carter in 1979.

In the early years, the Grand Ballroom had a high ceiling and included a balcony. Guests could stroll around the balcony and look out the upper windows at the ocean below. This was altered in 1960. Today, the Grand Ballroom serves as a theatrical and entertainment facility for conventions and as a ballroom for college fraternities and charity organizations. San Diegans love to transform the Grand Ballroom into a spectacular showplace with flowers, big band music and elegantly decorated tables.

There are those who believe the Hotel del Coronado was built merely to surround one of Southern California's most beautiful courtyards—and, they might be right! The Garden Patio is a popular retreat: guests can sit and enjoy the warm sun, couples can exchange wedding vows, and corporations can treat shareholders and clients to an elegant lawn reception. Interestingly enough, none of the many subtropical plants is indigenous to San Diego—all were introduced from abroad! Included among the beautiful flora are Mexican Guadalupe palms, a Brazilian Blue Jelly palm and Kenita palms from Australia's Lord Howe Island. There is a lonely male Cycad (a remnant of the prehistoric age).

The main attraction of the central courtyard is a wonderfully crafted gazebo, engineered by former hotel designer Dixon Morrow and constructed by staff car-

(Above): The newly renovated Prince of Wales Grill.

(Below): Hotel del Coronado's History Gallery on the lower level.

(Opposite, above): Sunset at The Del.

(Opposite, below): Hotel entrance.

penters. Morrow, who had been instrumental in restoring the hotel to its original state, discovered an early photograph of the Garden Patio which included a gazebo. Morrow went to work and designed a structure to match almost identically the one that had long since been torn down and forgotten. "Mr. (Larry) Lawrence is committed to restoring and keeping this old girl in as near original condition as possible and when I told him about the forgotten gazebo, he directed me to proceed with the construction of a new one," said Morrow. Today, unsuspecting visitors would never guess that the courtyard's gazebo is not original to the hotel. This is a tribute to the hotel craftsmen and to their ability to replicate woodwork which equals that of nineteenth century masters.

The hotel has accommodated history buffs by designating an entire lower passage as "The History Gallery." It is located at the west end of the Garden Patio and down one flight of stairs. This intriguing walk takes visitors back 100 years with displays of photos and architectural drawings of the hotel's construction, tools used in the construction, original electric lamps that Thomas Edison helped install, early hotel office and telephone equipment, as well as some cooking utensils. A large display of earlier photographs is located in the lower level on the east side of the hotel, beside the Del Deli.

The Deli is a most interesting place to eat; it has literally been carved out of what was once the hotel's rainwater storage cistern. (Not only did these huge concrete tanks supply the needs of the hotel but in the early days, they supplied the entire city of Coronado as well.) Doors connecting the various maze-like cistern rooms were cut with jackhammers through four-foot-thick concrete walls. Guests can easily see what an enormous task it was to create, but what a delightful place it is today! The Deli is open around-the-clock and serves sandwiches, salads, soups, beer, wine, and pastries.

Within full view of the ocean, visitors can dine alfresco at the Ocean Terrace. Offering California bistro fare, the Ocean Terrace serves up lunch and sunset appetizers, breakfast on weekends and holidays, and light dinner entrees May through October. Adjoining the Ocean Terrace is the Ocean Terrace Lounge, which offers live entertainment and dancing every night. Paneled in rich Philippine mahogany, its magnificent wooden bar was built in Pennsylvania in 1895 and shipped around Cape Horn to California. The ceiling is original.

The newest addition to The Del's dining facilities is the Prince of Wales Grill. The ocean front restaurant, which was recently renovated to reveal a romantic new look, was inspired by the "romance of the century." Legend has it that the Prince of Wales (who would later become King Edward VIII and then the Duke of Windsor) first saw Wallis Spencer Simpson during his visit to The Del in 1920. Sixteen years later he gave up his throne to marry the divorced Simpson. As the Duke and Duchess of Windsor, they became arbiters of elegance and glamour. Their timeless style is reflected in the new Prince of Wales Grill.

Directly below the Grand Ballroom is the International Room. At one time it was the stage for the famed performer, Liberace; the popular pianist performed here during the summers of 1949 and 1950 when it was known as the Circus Room. Other performers to appear in the old Circus Room were the "incomparable" Hildegard and the Ames Brothers. Today, the International Room serves as a ballroom, a meeting room or a banquet facility.

Back in the main lobby area, in what used to be the ladies' billiard room, is the Signature Shop, a full service lobby shop featuring The Del's signature collection of clothing, giftware and bath products. A wide array of periodicals and sundries is also available.

YESTERDAY'S

GRAND HOTEL TODAY AND TOMORROW

It is doubtful that anyone would plan an elegant Victorian structure in today's world, especially in Southern California where brass, glass and rustic wood are primary decor items. The Hotel del Coronado, to all outward appearances, belongs to a time when there were no automobiles, radios or television sets. The Del was born into an era when the telephone was a remote luxury and the incandescent light bulb was a new-fangled invention that probably wouldn't last. (There's proof of this in the hotel's History Gallery where an original electric light fixture is on display, complete with natural gas lamps which were built on each side of the bulb—just in case the electricity or the bulb failed!)

Edmund Wilson wrote in his 1931 book, "You feel that you can still enjoy here (at the Hotel del Coronado) the last moment before the power of American money...had finally turned its back altogether on the human tastes and habits of the old non-mechanical world."

But appearances are deceiving: the Hotel del Coronado has not only remained alive, it is constantly riding the crest of technology by offering the latest in hotel, restaurant and convention facilities. All of this has happened over the years because the private ownership, which has changed hands only five times in 100 years, has insisted that the hotel adapt itself to the demands of a changing world.

Back in 1888, when the hotel first opened, the latest technological innovation was the electric light. Thomas Edison himself traveled West to supervise the installation of his system into the hotel. The three Otis elevators, still in operation today, carry the serial numbers 061, 062 and 063; Otis has since built more that 2.5 million elevators. Another innovation of 1880s technology was an electric guest call and fire alarm system called an "annunciator." The installations of the annunciator and the electric light system were among the largest in the nation. The annunciator used 350 battery cells and 1900 pounds of copper wire. The incandescent light power plant, one of the first built in the state of California, boasted five Mather-type dynamos, two with a capacity to light 400 lights each and the other three capable of lighting 250 each. The Del's

(Above):The Hotel del Coronado's famed Dracaena Draco ("dragon tree") was planted in 1887, while the hotel was still being constructed. This rare liliaceous tree originates in China and the Canary Islands.

(Opposite): One of Southern California's most spectacular views can be found on the Promenade Deck, over-looking the ocean—a popular spot for catered parties. It overlooks the hotel's Olympic-sized pool, one of two pools at the hotel. The other is located by the Ocean Towers building.

installation of electrical lighting, the largest west of New York City, made major headlines in 1888. One newspaper account reported, "the mammoth building, illuminated with its hundreds of electric lights, presented a picture that will not easily be effaced from the memories of those who were present." Another news-paper story covered a fancy dress social ball, reporting that guests took time out from dancing in the Grand Ballroom to go down to the basement, through the tunnel, to the electric plant and inspect this modern-day marvel. As fascinating as the electric light was, there were still those guests who were dubious of its advan-tages. Each guest room had a small card prominently displayed, stating, "This room is equipped with the Edison Electric Light. Do not attempt to light with a match. Simply turn key on the wall by the door. The use of electricity for lighting is in no way harmful to health, nor does it affect soundness of sleep."

Today, the power plant is still directly across from the main entrance of the hotel. It is readily identifiable by the large smokestack which has been carefully preserved and is considered an important part of this National Historic Landmark.

The Hotel del Coronado is also cognizant of the world's need for energy conservation. To this end, the hotel maintains efficient energy production through its co-generation plant and solar power collection system. The Del has sixteen large solar collectors on the roof of the Grande Hall which pro-duce one percent of the hotel's electrical needs and five percent of its hot water. The hotel's solar photovoltaic system ensures that the backup batteries for the house computers are kept charged at all times. Additional hot water is produced by a heat harvesting system which captures waste heat from the air-conditioning system in the Ocean Towers complex, thus reducing natural gas consumption by about twenty-five percent. About one-third of the hotel's electricity is produced by an 800-kilowatt natural gas-fired turbine generator system below the Grande Hall. This co-generation system also supplies high pressure steam for the hotel's laundry facilities, the two spas, and the kitchens; the guest room heating, which is also sup-plied by this system, is recovered from hot exhaust gases.

THE BOATHOUSE

The Hotel del Coronado boathouse was built in 1887 for the enjoyment of the Hotel's guests. Pictured is the boathouse as it looked at the turn of the century with the now famous tent city. Guests from all around the world enjoyed everything the Del, tent city and the boathouse had to offer.

Today the Chart House restaurant occupies the historical Hotel del Coronado boathouse. In 1968, the Coronado boathouse was the third Chart House restaurant ever opened.

Below, the Boathouse as it looked in 1930.

A CITY WITHIN A CITY

The Del's kitchens alone have staff that could keep a number of small towns in America well fed. The staff is a good indication of just how many meals are served in any one twenty-four-hour period: there are two executive chefs, four sous chefs, seventy-six cooks, eight bakers, a butcher, a pastry chef, a wine steward, six hosts and hostesses, eleven captains, 113 servers, seventy-five busboys, eighteen bartenders, nine barboys and thirteen cocktail servers.

An average of 2500 meals a day come out of the central kitchen (large enough to contain two basketball courts). On special holidays, such as Thanksgiving and Christmas, that figure can rise to 6000 or more! The refrigerated food storage area in the lower level of the hotel covers nearly an acre. Breakfasts and lunches for the Ocean Terrace indoor and outdoor cafes are provided by the Prince of Wales kitchen because the gourmet restaurant is only open during dinner hours (5:30 p.m. to 10:30 p.m.).

The hotel's opening day photo of the Food and Beverage staff was recreated on the morning of February 19, 1988, the hotel's 100th birthday.

The hotel's security staff contains veteran police officers who, collectively, have more than 200 years of experience with local, state and federal agencies. The Coronado Police Department, which has a smaller number of officers, often calls upon the hotel's security department to assist them in such areas as language translation (more than twenty-four foreign languages are spoken by the huge staff).

The Del's maintenance department is one of the largest of any hotel in the world. There are twenty painters on the maintenance payroll alone; in addition, there are ten carpenters and assistants, assorted electricians and plumbers.

The hotel's laundry facility is one of the largest in San Diego County. Not only does it handle the bedding and dining room linens for the hotel, it also handles laundry needs for more than twenty other hotels and motels in the area.

Because of the unique decoration demands of the hotel (no two rooms of the main building are alike in size, shape or decoration), there is an upholstery shop. Its sole purpose is to recondition the hotel's furniture.

The carpentry shop provides handmade items to replace, match or add to those which cannot be obtained elsewhere.

Please Enjoy the Hotel del Coronado's Fine Restaurants and Lounges

CROWN-CORONET ROOM
Regional French Cuisine

Magnificent surroundings recall a more graceful era in the historic Crown-Coronet Room, where Sunday Brunch was voted "Best of the Best" in *San Diego Magazine*. Salads, seafood, and regional French cuisine. Breakfast, lunch, dinner, Sunday Brunch, Sunday dinner buffet with dancing. The Crown-Coronet Room is off the Main Lobby; for reservations, please dial extension 7240.

PRINCE OF WALES
An Ocean Front Grill

With charming candlelit tables and breathtaking views through panoramic windows, the Prince of Wales features vibrant culinary entrees, all grilled, pan-seared or broiled to perfection. Located on the lower Galleria Level. Reservations recommended; please dial extension 7240.

OCEAN TERRACE
California Bistro Fare Alfresco

Enjoy a view of the sparkling Pacific Ocean as you dine alfresco in the Ocean Terrace. California bistro fare; lunch and sunset appetizers, breakfast on weekends and holidays, light dinner entrees (May through October only). The Ocean Terrace is on the Galleria Level, overlooking the tennis courts. For reservations, please dial extension 7240.

DEL DELI
An Authentic New York-Style Delicatessen

For the best deli food this side of Manhattan, sample the authentic New York-style cuisine in the Del Deli, where traditional sandwiches are always piled sky high. Round-the-clock service; take-out and call-ahead orders. The Del Deli is on the lower Galleria Level; please dial extension 7293. ·

PALM COURT LOUNGE
On the Garden Patio

If you're looking for a refreshing break from the hustle and bustle of everyday life, stop by Palm Court for a light snack and a picturesque Garden Patio view. Coffee, cappuccino, espresso, fresh-baked croissants and pastries, cocktails and hors d'oeuvres. Piano accompaniment after 5 PM. Palm Court adjoins the Main Lobby; please dial extension 7275.

OCEAN TERRACE LOUNGE
Live Entertainment Nightly

Step up to the hand-carved, turn-of-the-century bar for cocktails and appetizers with a nostalgic twist. Live entertainment and dancing after 9 PM every night. The Ocean Terrace Lounge is on the lower Galleria Level; please dial extension 7279.

PROMENADE DECK BAR
Overlooking the Ocean

Enjoy a magnificent sunset view and a great margarita at the Promenade Deck Bar. Live entertainment Saturdays and Sundays during the summer; full bar. Open daily from 11:30 AM to dusk; overlooks the Main Pool; please dial extension 7413.

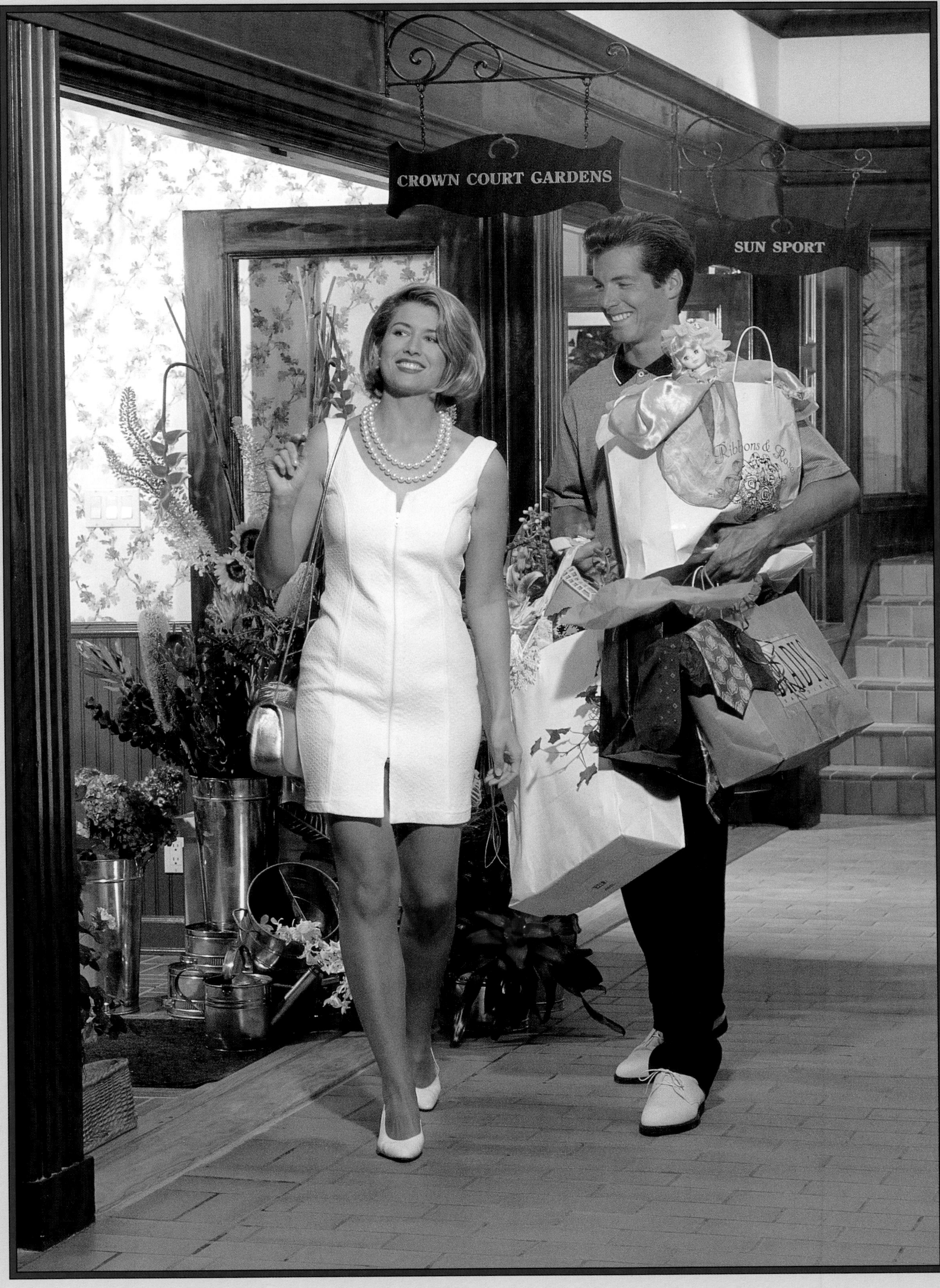
CROWN COURT GARDENS
SUN SPORT
Ribbons & Roses

Shops and Services

Apparel

BRADY'S FOR MEN
A complete collection of European-inspired contemporary clothing from classic suits to sportswear, including distinctive leather jackets, casual shoes and unique neckwear. Tuxedo rentals available. 437-1144 or ext. 7339

BRADY'S FOR WOMEN
A unique fashion boutique featuring many California designers in resort wear, cocktail dresses and novelty accessories in a full range of sizes. Also, Coronado's largest and most distinctive collection of designer swimwear. 435-6766 or ext. 7334

BUBBLES BEACHWEAR
A fun collection of clothing for active play at the beach, pool or even school! 522-8470 or ext. 7193

COURTSIDE
Upscale tennis apparel and active sportswear for on or off the courts. Racquets, shoes and accessories for the sports enthusiast. 435-6611 or ext. 7197

POOLSIDE
Provides all your last minute needs to ensure your comfort at the pool, featuring The Del's exclusive suncare products. Ext. 7350

RIBBONS AND ROSES
A collection of fine soaps, toiletries, elegant sleepwear, apparel and accessories in a romantic setting. 435-9270 or ext. 7165

SET SAIL
A classic collection of men's sportswear featuring an active, outdoor look. 435-6611 or ext. 7333

SPA BOUTIQUE
Located in our Health Spa, pamper yourself with one of our unique body treatments. While you're there, see the latest fashions in exercise wear. Ext. 7233

SUN SPORT
A unique viewpoint to the world of women's resort apparel featuring an innovative mix of prints and colors accented by a bright array of shoes and accessories. 435-6611 or ext. 7505

THE SWEATER STORE
Specializing in fine quality ladies' sweaters. Beautiful wool knits, cashmere, and a dazzling collection of beaded and jeweled sweaters. Also available, unique T-shirts and jackets. 435-8605 or ext. 7342

TROPICAL T'S
Bold and bright graphic T-shirts that reflect a California attitude, many with Hotel del Coronado logo. Accessories for beach, sun and fun. 435-6611 or ext. 7628

WAVES
Every day is a vacation featuring men's and women's island-inspired apparel. 435-6611 or ext. 7271

Art Galleries

THE CORONADO GALLERY
Large eclectic collection of graphic artwork beautifully framed and matted at reasonable prices. 435-4579 or ext. 7382

SUE TUSHINGHAM MCNARY ART GALLERY
Etchings and oils of San Diego artist Sue Tushingham McNary, as well as a wide variety of art, from affordable prints and posters to original paintings. 435-1819 or ext. 7505

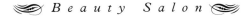

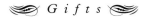
Beauty Salon

HOTEL DEL CORONADO HAIR DESIGNS
Full service salon for men and women. 437-4496 or ext. 7328

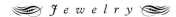
Gifts

NEW IMAGES
Presents functional electronic and educational items, gadgets and executive toys that stretch the imagination. Puzzles, novelty telephones, and travel accessories. 435-6039 or ext. 7380

THE RUFFLED DUCK
Country store features handcrafted wooden items, plaques, pottery, dolls and decorative accessories. 437-1500 or ext. 7627

SHELL WORLD
Custom designed shell and coral jewelry and nautical home decor items. Rare seashells from around the world. 437-1424 or ext. 7337

VICTORIAN CORNER
Unique gifts and collectibles, European crystal, antique silver, Lladro, Swarovski Royal Doulton, and Hummel. 435-9131 or ext. 7338

Jewelry

DEL CORONADO JEWELS, INC.
Family owned for two generations, since 1951. Specializing in "crown" jewelry. Cubic zirconia and synthetic stones in 14kt mountings. The finest in affordable jewelry in many price ranges. 435-6061 or ext. 7340

GEORGE CARTER JESSOP JEWELERS
Fine jewelry–new and estate. Gemstones, pearls, custom design and jewelry repair. Rolex watches, sales and service. San Diego's oldest family of fine jewelers. 437-1707 or ext. 7329

OPALS AND GEMS OF AUSTRALIA
Australia's internationally renowned jeweler, specializing in gem quality opals, opal jewelry and rare exotic gems direct from our mines. 435-1184 or ext. 7597

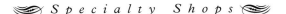
Specialty Shops

AMERICAN NOSTALGIA
A '50s style store featuring classic vintage Coca-Cola and Marilyn Monroe memorabilia. 437-4969 or ext. 7332

EUROPEAN HERITAGE
North America's largest producer of European heraldry, including coats of arms, calligraphy, embroideries and monograms. 435-3909 or ext. 7341

GEPPETTO'S
Unusual playthings for imaginative infants and children. Toys, games, books, dolls, beach toys and T-shirts. 435-8871 or ext. 7330

HOTEL DEL CORONADO SIGNATURE SHOP
Full service lobby shop featuring our signature collection of clothing, giftware, and bath products. Also available, a wide array of periodicals and sundries. 435-6611 or ext. 7274

SALLY HUSS GALLERY
A lively collection of art that is happy in nature and free-spirited in style depicted in serigraphs, fun gift art, greeting cards, jewelry, clothing and more. 435-9185 or ext. 7424

SUNGLASS HUT
The largest selection of sunglasses in Southern California at the lowest prices. 522-0245 or ext. 8480

WINDSOR CHOCOLATES
Reminiscent of an old-fashioned candy store, with a selection of handmade chocolates, fudge, salt water taffy, jelly beans and other popular sweets, including sugar free items. 437-4121 or ext. 7320

Coronado Tent City.

HOTEL DEL CORONADO
HAS BEEN DESIGNATED A
NATIONAL
HISTORIC LANDMARK
THIS SITE POSSESSES NATIONAL SIGNIFICANCE
IN COMMEMORATING THE HISTORY OF THE
UNITED STATES OF AMERICA
1977
NATIONAL PARK SERVICE
UNITED STATES DEPARTMENT OF THE INTERIOR

CORONADO HISTORICAL
LANDMARK
HOTEL DEL CORONADO—1888
DEDICATED 1972
CORONADO HISTORICAL ASSOCIATION

M. Larry Lawrence, owner of the Hotel del Coronado, has pioneered the renaissance of this Victorian treasure. His $80 million restoration project has resulted in the hotel's designation as a National Historic Landmark.

The original entrance of the Hotel del Coronado as it is approached from the south up the Silver Strand—many years before anyone thought about building a bridge across the San Diego Bay.

CHRONOLOGY

1769—Mission San Diego de Acalá founded

1846—Don Pedro Carrillo sells Coronado peninsula for $1,000

1869—Coronado peninsula sold again, this time for $10,000

1885—Babcock & Story buy Coronado peninsula for $110,000

1886—First 4th of July Celebration at the Del

1887—March groundbreaking is held for the new Hotel del Coronado

1888—First guest checks into The Del on February 19

1891—Benjamin Harrison is first U.S. president to stay at The Del

1900—John D. Spreckels becomes second owner of Hotel del Coronado

1904—Thomas Edison dedicates hotel's first lighted Christmas tree

1909—San Diego's first Charity Ball held at the Hotel del Coronado

1919—President Woodrow Wilson rests at the Hotel del Coronado

1920—Britain's Prince of Wales fêted in The Crown Room

1927—Some 1,100 citizens honor Charles Lindbergh in The Crown Room

MGM films *The Flying Fleet*, starring Ramon Navarro, at The Del

1935—President Franklin Roosevelt makes the first of many visits to hotel

1942—U.S. Navy takes portions of The Del as officer quarters during WWII

1948—The Hotel del Coronado sold twice within 48 hours

1958—Director Billy Wilder films his famed *Some Like It Hot* at The Del

1960—President Dwight Eisenhower stays at the Hotel del Coronado

1961—John Alessio becomes fifth owner of the Hotel del Coronado

1963—M. Larry Lawrence, Chairman of the Board, becomes the hotel's sixth and present owner

1970—President Nixon hosts Mexican president, former President Johnson at hotel

1977—U.S. Department of Interior designates The Del a "National Historic Landmark"

1979—President Jimmy Carter fêted at hotel by San Diego civic leaders

1982—President Reagan hosts Mexican President De la Madrid at The Del

1984—Billy Wilder honored by hotel for 25th anniversary of *Some Like It Hot*

1986—Sail America Party and Hotel del Coronado's 98th birthday

1988—Hotel del Coronado Centennial

1991—Mexican President Carlos Salinas de Gortari visits the Del

1993—President Bill Clinton visits the Hotel del Coronado

A LIVING LEGEND

A CELEBRATION OF THE DEL

BEACHFRONT RESORT The Hotel del Coronado is the largest full-service beachfront resort on the North American Pacific Coast. From Anchorage to Acapulco, there is no other facility that equals the grandeur, the elegance or the service provided by The Del. Guests can enjoy the Pacific surf outside their guest rooms or suite windows. But most guests don't just come to look out their windows; they come to walk and to play on the wonderful white sandy beach, to play tennis on one of the six lighted hard courts, to swim in the Olympic-size swimming pool, to surf, to fish or to rent a sailboat at nearby Glorietta Bay, or to golf on the finely manicured fairways and greens of the Coronado Golf Course, which is just a few short blocks (within walking distance) from the hotel.

TENNIS The Del is regularly included on lists of the world's finest tennis resorts. Frequently top professional stars, such as Chris Evert, stop by for a relaxing weekend of beach and sun and, of course, to play a couple of sets of tennis with Ben Press, the popular hotel pro. (The City of Coronado provides an additional fourteen tennis courts to supplement those at The Del.) Tennis buffs will find the game a bit different here. The nearby ocean puts moisture on the ball, making the game a little slower, but more of a challenge!

GOLF As mentioned, the Coronado Golf Course is located conveniently nearby, but there are a number of other fine courses throughout San Diego County. Torrey Pines, north of La Jolla, is the site of the annual San Diego Open. This is just one of more than fifty courses in the greater San Diego area.

BOATING Sailboating is a popular nautical sport. But if this isn't quite your cup of tea, a cruise around San Diego Bay in a harbor excursion boat is a calmer alternative. Or you can opt for one of the whale-watching boats, which go out to the open sea and travel alongside migrating grey whales (seasonal).

SAN DIEGO Landlubbers enjoy San Diego for its world famous San Diego Zoo. But the city also offers the Wild Animal Park, Sea World and cultural attractions such as the Old Globe Theater located in beautiful Balboa Park. Besides the Old Globe, Balboa Park offers a number of fine museums, including the Aerospace Museum (which displays a collection of vintage aircraft) and the Reuben E. Fleet Space Theater. San Diego also has a fine opera company, and symphony and pop orchestras that give regularly scheduled performances throughout the year. There are also more than thirty community playhouses in San Diego County, including the Coronado Playhouse, which is less than four blocks from the hotel!

TIJUANA The Hotel del Coronado is also less than ten miles from the most visited city in the world. Once considered a dusty, sailor's bar-hopping retreat, Tijuana today is Mexico's fourth largest city with a population of more than 1.3 million (second only to Los Angeles along the North American Pacific coast). More than 42 million people cross the international border between San Diego and Tijuana each year. Going to Tijuana is one of the most popular day trips of hotel guests. They go for the shopping bargains of leather goods, pottery, jewelry and clothing, and also because of the growing number of fine restaurants offering international cuisines.

CONVENTIONS Over the past several years, the Hotel del Coronado has become known as one of the West's great meeting and convention facilities. Hundreds of groups, both large and small, take advantage of the hotel's complete list of services. The Del has thirty meeting and banquet rooms which accommodate from twenty-five to 1500 people. The Grande Hall convention center can be subdivided into three individual soundproof rooms, each holding up to 500 persons: Regent, Empress and Viceroy Halls. Other large meeting rooms include the International Room, directly below the Grand Ballroom (400 persons), and the magnificent Crown Room, which can accommodate up to 1000 people for group dining.